For all the children in the world

For our darling son Isaiah,

our God children,

his cousins,

and

all the children in the world.

"Love always overcomes fear"

Our hearts will love you forevermore

Published by Aunty Lolly Books 2023
Blessings With Love, For You, We Pray
Text Copyright © 2022 Lauren Lee Byrne Allan
Illustration Copyright © 2022 Lauren Lee Byrne Allan
Printed in Australia

All inquiries should be directed to
www.auntylollybooks.com

ISBN 978-0-473-64902-9
ISBN 978-0-473-64903-6
ISBN 978-0-473-64905-0

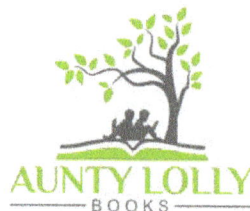

AUNTY LOLLY
BOOKS

Blessings With Love, For You, We Pray

Written by Lauren Lee Byrne Allan

Illustrated by Jezreel Cuevas

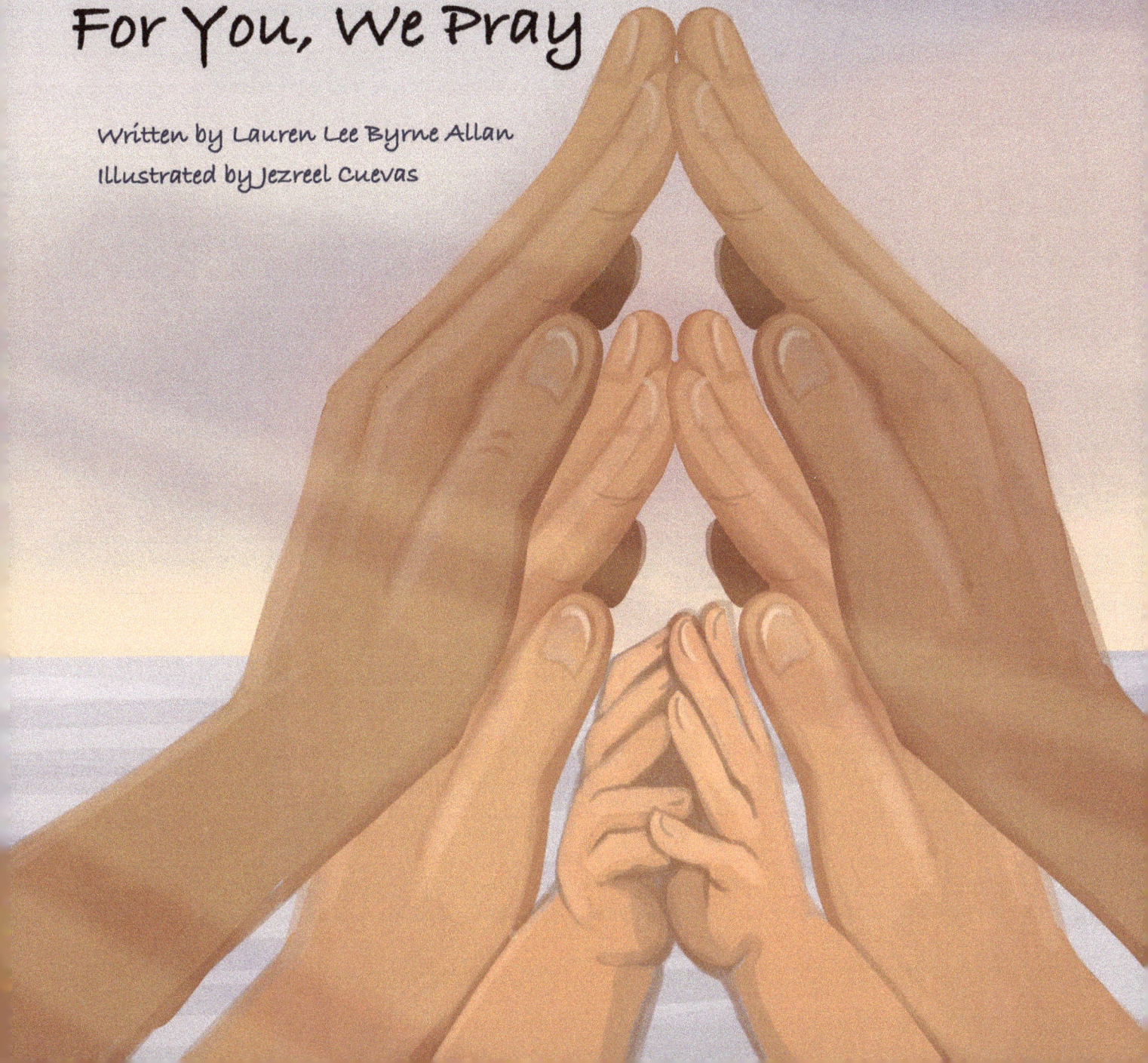

We loved and prayed for you before you were born

That you would come into this world healthy and warm

For You,
We Pray

Your spirit is full of true love, peace and grace

While you always know with God, you have a very special place

Divine blessings
will give you a
most wonderful life

Full of goodness and joy
so you will thrive

From clarity and wisdom, you will do what is right

A moral compass that offers salvation, protection and might

Your heart will be beautiful, caring and kind

Which will shine brightly to all of life's kind

You live with respect, calm and unity

With love, be your best person in any community

You will be confident,
secure and safe

So, with a healthy
self-esteem, there will be
nothing you cannot face

You are blessed with well-being and health

Honoured as two of your greatest forms of wealth

You see hope and beauty in all that you do

Recognise your uniqueness and always remain true

You are grateful, forgiving and thankful all in one

While living in harmony,

you know

all your growing will continue to be done

You appreciate your life and live it as a treasured gift

So, in moments of trial, you have an extraordinary lift

Believe in God and yourself every single day

Share your hope, gifts and talents in your own special way

For You,
We Pray
Amen

A WORD BY THE AUTHOR

Dear Reader,

Your kind feedback is very important,

and your voice is genuinely valued.

If you enjoyed this book,

please take a minute to leave a review.

Thank you so much.

Much appreciated and warm regards,

Lauren

ABOUT THE AUTHOR

Lauren has always loved storytelling
and, as a child, dreamed
of being a writer when she grew up.

On her way to becoming an author,
she has been a teacher to hundreds
of children across the world.

She loves to write meaningful stories
encouraging the positive growth
of children's hearts and minds.

She says, "Follow your heart, believe in your dreams
and build upon them because they can
also come true for you!"

Find Lauren at
www.auntylollybooks.com

OTHER TRANSLATED WORKS OF THIS BOOK

Ngā Manaakitanga I roto I te Aroha,
Mōu, E Īnoī Ana Tātou

Bendiciones de Amor:
Por ti, rezamos

www.ingramcontent.com/pod-product-compliance
Lightning Source LLC
Chambersburg PA
CBHW040249100426
42811CB00011B/1208